Zeb's First Christmas

Title: The Adventures of Zebulon of the Airborne Rangers
Subtitle: Zeb's First Christmas

ISBN: 978-1-7369295-4-4 (Paperback)
ISBN: 978-1-7369295-5-1 (Hardcover)

Written by Sharon Burton
Illustrated by Ciena Hanahan

www.TheAdventuresOfZeb.com

The Adventures of Zebulon of the Airborne Rangers

Collect the series!

Book 1: Welcome Home

Book 2: The Big Blue Monster

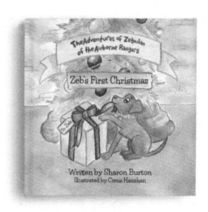

Book 3: Zeb's First Christmas

It was fall in Colorado Springs.

My favorite season of the year!

1

The leaves turned yellow and blew
down on the ground.

We all helped Dad rake leaves.
It was so much fun!

3

Soon all the leaves were gone.

I started sleeping on my warm bed
in the garage.

5

My brothers and sisters got new clothes, pencils, rulers and lots of interesting things.

One day my brothers and sisters got up early and went away in a big, yellow bus.

I waited and waited for them.

I was so excited every day when they came home.

Then we would play and play.

Mom said I was bored and lonely, so she bought me toys to play with.

I kept running out of toys! They all disappeared!

Finally, Mom and Dad bought me a very special toy. It was the best red ball ever in the world.

Mom said that an elephant could not destroy it!

13

One morning I woke up to a wonderful smell.

Mom was already in the kitchen.

15

I stayed there for a long time helping her keep the kitchen clean!

A little later lots of people called relatives came over.

They brought more food and we had
a big feast!

18

Then we watched football.

That night, Mom put something special in my food.
She called it turkey and gravy.

It was the best day ever!

A few days later...

One night it got very cold. I curled in a tight ball
on my bed in the garage.

24

The next morning everything was different!
There was white, wet stuff everywhere!

It was called snow.

I jumped in it!

I rolled in it!

I ate it!

I played with my brothers and sisters in it!

It was almost winter.

My favorite season of the year!

I was so tired that night.
I had happy dreams about snow.

Christmas...

Something exciting was happening!

Mom and Dad brought boxes and bags and hid them in the garage.

My Mom made a big play area for me in the living room.

She filled it with paper and curly ribbons.

A few days later, Dad brought home something special for me. He called it a pulling harness. It fit perfectly!

Then he put ropes on the harness and tied them to a snow saucer.

I gave my brother, Mike, a ride on the sled!

Ahhhhh!

We had so much fun!

Dad said we needed to get a Christmas tree. I love trees!

No one wanted to go with Dad because there was too much snow in the mountains. I wanted to go!

It was just Dad and me in the truck.

When we got to the tree cutting area, I jumped out of the truck.

I chased pinecones.

I sniffed in the snow.

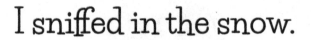

Dad threw sticks for me.
I found some of them.

Dad looked at a lot of trees. He found a tree he said was perfect. Then he cut it down for me!

40

It smelled very good. I tugged on the branches and started dragging it. It was my tree!

Dad put the harness on me, then put a rope around his waist. He helped me pull my tree back to the truck!

When we got home, Dad showed everyone my tree!

He trimmed the end of the tree trunk and put it in a stand.

He gave me a piece of the tree trunk and I took it to my bed in the garage that night. It was the best day ever!

A few weeks later...

Tinkle, tinkle...
Jingle, jingle...

One night a strange thing happened. I woke up and heard noises outside. I heard bells tinkling.

It was very dark in the garage, but I heard someone say,

"Who is a good dog?
You are, Zeb!
Ho! Ho! Ho!"

47

The next morning Mom brought me in the house. The Christmas tree had boxes underneath it. My brothers and sisters were very excited. I picked up a box but Mom make me put it down.

48

I had so much fun watching everyone open their presents.
I got a present too! It was a bone almost as big as me!

When we were done I watched Mom put something in the oven that smelled really good. It wasn't turkey this time. I hoped I would get to taste it.

Mom's dinner was amazing! She gave me two, big meaty bones!
They were yummy good! Then we watched a movie together.

When the movie was over, Mom and Dad went into the garage and
Mom came back holding something. It was moving!

All of my siblings ran over to see it. I stood on my hind legs
but could not see it! What was it?

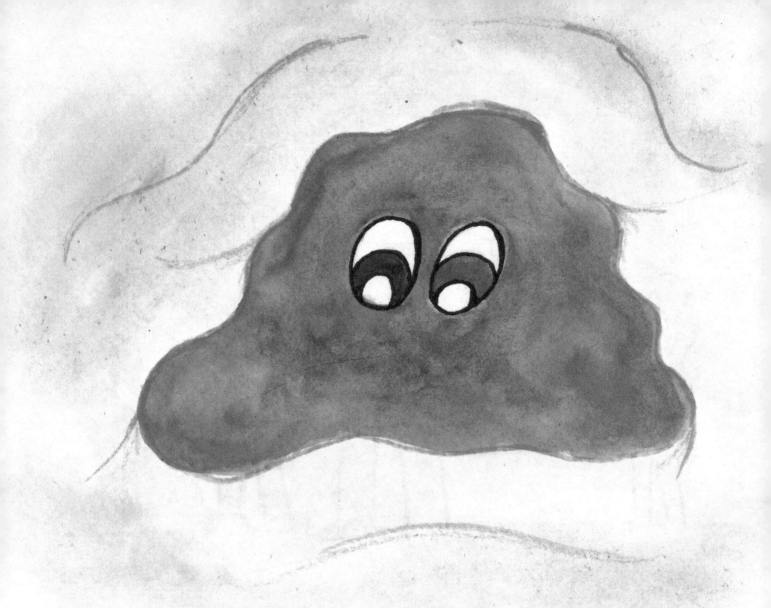

Mom bent down and showed me, wrapped in a blanket
was an... Oh my!

MOM AND DAD GOT ME A PUPPY FOR CHRISTMAS!!!

Everyone was so excited for me! My siblings were all trying to think of names for him.

Mom said he was a Collie. I tried to tell everyone that I wanted to name him Woof!

Mom said she had already picked a name using his dog Dad's name, Sir Sid. She named him Sir Sid's Son Samson, but we were going to call him Sam.

We played with Sam the rest of the evening, then
Mom made a special, warm bed for him in the garage.

It was such an exciting day and I was so tired that I lay down in my bed to look at my puppy. I yawned like a roaring lion and then my eyes started to close.

It was the best day...ev...ZZZZZZ.

61

Sharon & Lee

Zeb

Rachel   Allyson   Stephen   Mike

To join Zeb on more adventures, visit:

www.TheAdventuresOfZeb.com

Zebulon of the Airborne Rangers 1989-2003;
Chesapeake Bay Retriever extraordinaire.

Zeb was a special dog. We didn't know it then.

It did not matter if he was working or playing. He lived life large, in the moment and with a heart fully committed to everything he did.

I wanted to be like Zeb.

Zeb left us with many remarkable memories. I decided to share his stories in the hope you will enjoy them as much as we still do. They are all true.

~ The Burtons ~

Made in the USA
Monee, IL
06 January 2024

48974169R00044